Believe · Celebrate · Live™

Reconciliation

Preparing to Celebrate First Penance

W9-CPQ-198

The Subcommittee on the Catechism, United States Conference of Catholic Bishops, has found this text, copyright 2017, to be in conformity with the *Catechism of the Catholic Church*.

S® Sadlier Religion

Believe • Celebrate • Live™
...developed by the community of faith through...

Catechetical and Liturgical Consultants
Carole M. Eipers, D.Min.
National Catechetical Advisor
William H. Sadlier, Inc.

Donna Eschenauer, Ph.D.
Associate Dean
Associate Professor, Pastoral Theology
St. Joseph's Seminary
Yonkers, NY

Matthew Halbach, Ph.D.
St. Joseph Educational Center
West Des Moines, IA

Tom Kendzia, B.Mus.Ed.
Composer and Director of Music
Christ the King Parish
Kingston, RI

Barbara Sutton, D.Min.
Associate Dean of Ministerial
   Formation and Outreach
St. John's School of Theology and Seminary
Collegeville, MN

Theological Consultants
Most Reverend Edward K. Braxton,
   Ph.D., S.T.D.
Official Theological Consultant
Bishop of Belleville

Monsignor John E. Pollard, S.T.L.
Pastor, Queen of All Saints Basilica
Chicago, IL

Reverend Donald Senior, CP, Ph.D., S.T.D.
Member, Pontifical Biblical Commission
President Emeritus of Catholic Theological
   Union
Chicago, IL.

Inculturation Consultants
C. Vanessa White, Ph.D.
Catholic Theological Union
Chicago, IL

Dulce M. Jiménez-Abreu
Director of Bilingual Religion Markets
William H. Sadlier, Inc.

Luis J. Medina, M.A.
Bilingual Consultant
St. Louis, MO

Curriculum and Child Development Consultant
Thomas S. Quinlan, M.Div.
Director, Religious Education Office
Diocese of Joliet

Special Needs Consultants
Charleen Katra, M.A.
Associate Director Specializing in
   Disability Ministry
Archdiocese of Galveston-Houston

Madonna Wojtaszek-Healy, Ph.D.
Consultant for Special Needs, Religious
   Education Office
Diocese of Joliet

Media/Technology Consultant
Spirit Juice Studios
Chicago, IL

Sadlier Consulting Team
Suzan Larroquette
Director of Catechetical Consultant
   Services

Kathy Hendricks
National Catechetical Consultant

Timothy R. Regan
Regional Vice President

Writing/Development Team
Diane Lampitt, M.Ed.
Vice President, Product Management,
   Religion

Alexandra Rivas-Smith
Executive Vice President, Product
   Management

Mary Carol Kendzia
Research and Development Director,
   Religion

Joanne McDonald
Editorial Director

Regina Kelly
Supervising Editor

William M. Ippolito
Director of Corporate Planning

Editors
Ellen Marconi, Dignory Reina, Gloria
Shahin, Robert Vigneri

Publishing Operations Team
Blake Bergen
Vice President, Publications

Carole Uettwiller
Vice President of Planning and Technology

Robert Methven
Vice President, Digital Publisher

Vince Gallo
Senior Creative Director

Francesca O'Malley
Art/Design Director

Cesar Llacuna
Senior Image Manager

Cheryl Golding
Production Director

Monica Reece
Senior Production Manager

Jovito Pagkalinawan
Electronic Prepress Director

Martin Smith
Planning and Analysis Project Director

Yolanda Miley
Accounts and Permissions Director

Lucy Rotondi
Business Manager

Design/Image Staff
Kevin Butler, Nancy Figueiredo, Stephen Flanagan, Lorraine
Forte, Debrah Kaiser, Gabriel Ricci, Bob Schatz, Karen Tully

Production Staff
Robin D'Amato, Carol Lin, Vincent McDonough, Allison
Pagkalinawan, Laura Reischour

Photo Credits
age fotostock/CSP_monkeybusiness: 63; KidStock: 77. Alamy
Stock Photo/Tony Eveling: 9. Corbis/Alloy: 78; Michael Pole: 15
bottom; Wavebreak Media Ltd.: 15 *top*, 20 *bottom*. The Crosiers/
Gene Plaisted, OSC: 57. Dreamstime.com/Jojjik: 65; R. Gino
Santa Maria/Shutterfree Llc: 94 *top*; Thorken: 28. Fotolia/
Stefano Garau: 94 *top*; goodween123: 21 *background*; Dmitry
Pichugin: 51; SSilver: 79; WavebreakMediaMicro: 13 *top*. Getty
Images/Gary S. Chapman: 84 *center left*; Comstock Images: 14
bottom; KidStock: 41, 48 *top*; Ariel Skelley: 35. GoodSalt/Darrel
M Tank: 26, 34 *top*. iStock/artpipi: 84 *top*; Pamela Moore: 40
bottom. Shutterstock.com/5 second Studio: 23; Artspace: 46;
Mikkel Bigandt: 37; Jillian Cain: 83 *background*, 90 *bottom
background*; Cienpies Design: 60; JuliRose: 18; Neil Lang: 74;
Matvienko Vladimir: 88; Proskurina Yuliya: 32; Zurijeta: 13
bottom; zzveillust: 86 *bottom*. Spirit Juice Studios: 6, 8, 12, 16,
20 *top*, 22, 27, 29, 30, 34 *bottom*, 36, 42, 43, 44, 48 *bottom*,
50, 54, 55, 56, 58, 62, 64, 68, 69, 70, 72, 76, 78, 84 *left*, 84
right, 84 *center right*, 85 *left*, 85 *right*, 86 *top*. SuperStock/
Blend Images: 14 *top*, 82, 83, 85 *center*, 90 *top*, 90 *bottom*;
Exactostock: 94 *bottom*; Fancy Collection: 21, 40 *top*; Loop
Images: 93 *bottom*; Ariel Skelley: 49.

Illustrator Credits
Bob Kayganich: 4-5. Kelley McMorris: 10-11, 19, 24-25, 33,
38-39, 47, 52-53, 61, 66-67, 75, 80-81, 89. Zina Saunders:
17, 31, 45, 59, 73, 87.

Nihil Obstat
Rev. Matthew S. Ernest, S.T.D.
Rev. Kevin J. O'Reilly, S.T.D.
Censores Librorum

Imprimatur
✠ His Eminence, Timothy Cardinal Dolan
Archbishop of New York
May 12, 2017

The *Nihil Obstat* and *Imprimatur* are official declarations
that a book or pamphlet is free of doctrinal or moral error.
No implication is contained therein that those who have
granted the *Nihil Obstat* and *Imprimatur* agree with the
contents, opinions, or statements expressed.

Acknowledgments
Excerpts from the English translation of *The Roman Missal*
© 2010, International Committee on English in the Liturgy,
Inc. (ICEL). All rights reserved.

Scripture excerpts are taken from the *New American Bible
with Revised New Testament and Psalms*. Copyright © 1991,
1986, 1970, Confraternity of Christian Doctrine, Inc.
Washington, D.C. Used with permission. All rights reserved.
No part of the *New American Bible* may be reproduced by
any means without permission in writing from the
copyright owner.

Excerpts from the English translation of the *Catechism of the
Catholic Church* for the United States of America, copyright
© 1994, United States Catholic Conference, Inc.—Libreria
Editrice Vaticana. English translation of the *Catechism of the
Catholic Church: Modifications from the Editio Typica* copyright
© 1997, United States Catholic Conference, Inc.—Libreria
Editrice Vaticana. Used with permission.

Excerpts from the English translation of *Rite of Baptism for
Children* © 1969, ICEL; excerpts from the English translation
of the *Rite of Penance* © 1974, ICEL. All rights reserved.

Excerpts from *Catholic Household Blessings and Prayers
(Revised Edition)* © 1988, 2007, United States Conference of
Catholic Bishops, Washington, D.C. Used with permission.
All rights reserved.

English translation of the Glory Be to the Father and Lord's
Prayer by the International Consultation on English Texts
(ICET).

"Answer the Call" © 2011, Tom Kendzia. Published by
OCP, 5536 NE Hassalo, Portland, OR 97213. All rights
reserved. "Remember Your Love" text by Mike Balhoff,
music by Darryl Ducote and Gary Daigle, Copyright
© 1978, Damean Music, GIA Publications, Inc., agent, 7404
S. Mason Ave., Chicago, IL 60638 • www.giamusic.com •
800.442.1358. All rights reserved. Used by permission.
"Change Our Hearts" Text and music: Rory Cooney, ©
1984, OCP, 5536 NE Hassalo, Portland, OR 97213. All rights
reserved. "Open My Eyes" © 1988 Jesse Manibusan.
Published by Spirit & Song, a division of OCP. 5536 NE
Hassalo, Portland, OR 97213. All rights reserved. Used with
permission. *Healing Balm* by Peter M. Kolar: Copyright
© 2004, World Library Publications, wlpmusic.com. All
rights reserved. Used by permission. *I Send You Out* by John
Angotti: Copyright © 2000, World Library Publications,
wlpmusic.com. All rights reserved. Used by permission.

Contents

In our church there are different places where we might go to confession.

Welcome

This is a time of great joy for you and your family as you prepare to celebrate the Sacrament of Penance for the first time. There will be many people to guide you on your journey with Jesus. The whole parish community is praying for you.

As you go through each chapter:

Believe

You will recognize God's presence in your life as you recall your stories and as you see and hear the Word of God in the Scripture stories.

Celebrate

You will learn about the Church's celebration of the Sacrament of Penance and Reconciliation as you prepare to celebrate your First Penance.

Live

You will respond to God's grace by continuing to grow as a disciple of Jesus Christ.

May you always recognize God's action and presence in your life!

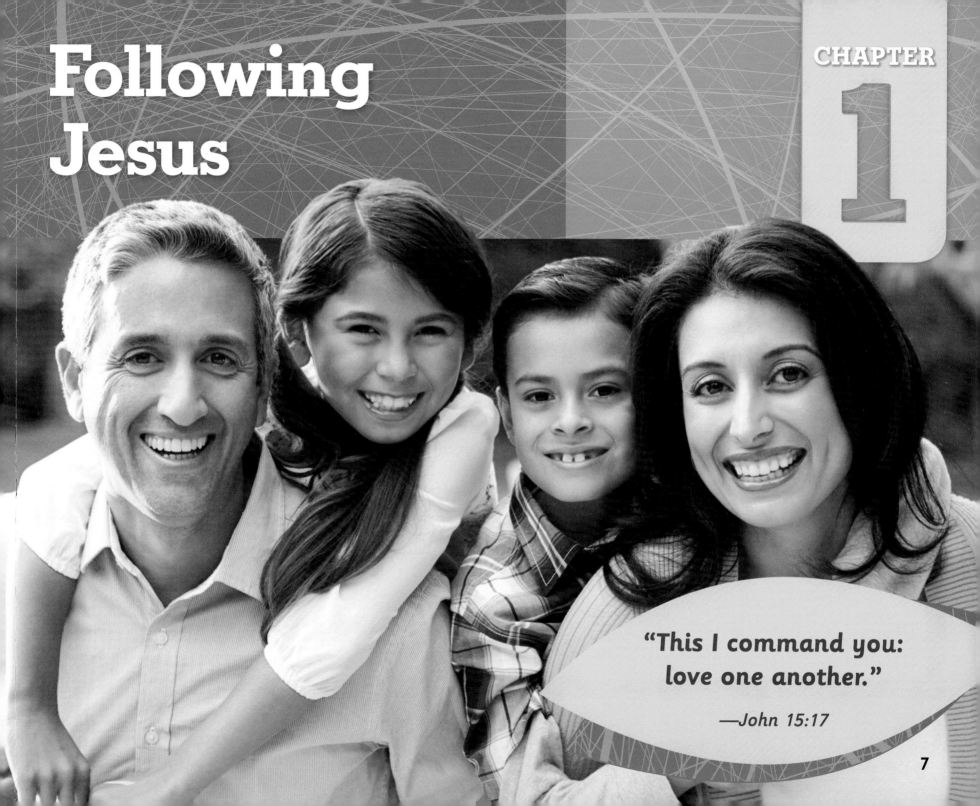

Following Jesus

CHAPTER 1

"This I command you: love one another."

—John 15:17

Believe

Open Your Heart

People Who Love and Care for Me

A Path of Love

Imagine you are hiking a long path. The path is not easy. It is uphill. You have to be careful. You must climb over rocks and branches. But beautiful flowers line the path. Sun shines through tall, green trees. Birds are chirping. And walking ahead of you is Jesus. He says, "Come, follow me."

Living as a disciple of Jesus is like hiking this path. Sometimes it is not easy. You might make a wrong choice. You might stumble and fall. But Jesus shows you the way. He is the Son of God, and he wants to show you how to live as God's child. He teaches you ways to treat others with kindness and love, which we call charity.

What are some examples of charity in your family, school, neighborhood, or parish?

"This is the path of charity, that is, of the love of God and of neighbor."

—*Catechism of the Catholic Church*, 1889

Believe

The Word of the Lord

We believe in the Blessed Trinity, the Three Persons in One God: God the Father, God the Son, God the Holy Spirit. Jesus is God the Son. He taught that, because God the Father loves us and wants to protect us, God gave us good laws to follow. Jesus taught us that the Holy Spirit would help us to follow and obey God's laws. God's laws are called commandments. Jesus taught us that by following God's commandments we show our love for God, others, and ourselves.

 Based on MATTHEW 22:35–39

Jesus went from town to town to tell people about God's special love. One day Jesus was asked which commandment is the greatest. Jesus said, "You shall love the Lord, your God, with all your heart, with all your soul, and with all your mind." Then he said, "You shall love your neighbor as yourself" (Matthew 22:37, 39).

We call this teaching of Jesus the *Great Commandment*.

The Ten Commandments

God gave special laws to his people because he loved them very much. He wanted his people to be safe and happy. The **Ten Commandments** are Laws given to us by God.

When Jesus was growing up, he learned the Ten Commandments. He lived by these laws all during his life on earth. He showed us how to follow and keep these laws. He taught us how to love God, others, and ourselves.

Here are ways we can show our love for God by following the First through Third Commandments.

1. We believe that there is only One God.

2. We speak God's name only with reverence, or honor and respect. We honor and respect the names of Jesus, Mary, and all the saints.

3. We join our parish each week for Mass on Sunday, the Lord's Day, which begins on Saturday evening. We take time to rest and enjoy our family and friends on the Lord's Day.

CATHOLIC IDENTITY
The commandments help us to live as God's children.

We follow the Third Commandment by participating in the celebration of the Eucharist (Mass) on Sunday.

Here are ways we can show love for others and ourselves by following the Fourth through Tenth Commandments:

4. We listen to and obey our parents and all those who care for us.

5. We respect all human life. We do not fight or hurt anyone.

6. We respect our bodies and the bodies of others.

7. We take care of what we have. We do not steal what other people have.

8. We tell the truth. We do not gossip or tell lies about others.

9. We show that we are thankful for our own family and friends. We are pure of heart and show love in an honest and faithful way.

10. We show that we are thankful for what we have. We are not jealous of what others have.

Jesus' teaching about loving God, others, and ourselves is called the **Great Commandment**. When we follow the Great Commandment, we follow all of God's commandments. We live as God's children.

We follow the Sixth Commandment by respecting our bodies.

We follow the Seventh Commandment by taking care of what we have.

Making Moral Choices

Jesus taught us to show love for God, others, and ourselves. God wants us to choose to obey his laws as Jesus taught us to do. Yet God never forces us to obey his commandments. God gives us the gift of **free will**. This gift allows us to make our own choices.

God lets us use our free will to follow his laws or not to follow his laws. God allows us to choose to love and respect him, others, and ourselves.

We live as God's children when we show reverence for God and love and respect for others and ourselves.

14

There are some things that we must never choose because they are always wrong, or evil. We must never choose to do unloving things, even if we think good might come from them.

Every day we make choices. Sometimes we must make a **moral choice**, a choice between right and wrong. Before making a choice, we should stop and ask ourselves:

- If I do this, will I show love for God, others, and myself?
- What would Jesus want me to do?
- How do God's laws help me to decide what to do?

Before you make a moral choice, ask yourself: Does this action show love for God, others, and myself? What would Jesus want me to do?

God has given us a gift to help us make the right choices. God has given us a conscience. Our **conscience** helps us to know what is right and what is wrong, what to do and what not to do. Our conscience helps us to obey God's laws.

Sometimes people choose to turn away from God's love. They decide not to follow and obey God's laws. When they do this they hurt their friendship with God. It is important to remember that God always loves us and is ready to forgive us if we are sorry and want to do better. God gives us the help we need, the gift of **grace**, to do what he commands. We can pray to God the Holy Spirit to help us make the right choices.

Live

Become What You Believe

I show love and reverence for God and respect for others . . .

in my home:

_____
_____
_____

at school:

_____
_____
_____

in my neighborhood:

_____
_____
_____

I follow and obey God's commandments by showing love and respect for others!

Discipleship in Action

Saint Andrew Kim Taegŏn (1821–1846)

Andrew Kim Taegŏn was from Korea. He was baptized a Catholic when he was fifteen years old. Later he traveled more than a thousand miles to China to become a priest. Andrew became the first priest and pastor in Korea. Father Andrew helped and cared for many people. He helped Korean Christians to escape to China. At that time, the Church was not allowed in Korea. Father Andrew tried to bring missionaries there. Because of his faith and work for the Church, he was captured and killed. At his death, he said everything he did, he did for God. He wanted other people to know the love of God.

I can help people to know the love of God. Today I will do this by . . .

Live

Answer the Call

Leader: Let us pray the Sign of the Cross.

Loving God, you call us to love you above all things and to love one another as we love ourselves. In Baptism you call us by name and send us to be signs of your love. We join now in singing a song reminding us to live the Great Commandment.

All: (*Refrain*) With faith in our hearts, we answer the call,
to love one another, be hope and peace for all.
From the waters of life, we are sent to be light,
to break through the darkness,
to answer the call of God.

Leader: We ask the Holy Spirit to help us to answer the call to love God and one another.

All: (*Sing refrain.*)

Leader: Come forward to bless yourselves with the holy water from the bowl. Let this water remind us of our Baptism, as we ask Jesus to help us to answer the call of God.

All: (*Sing refrain.*)

Leader: Let us fold our hands and pray as Jesus taught us.

All: Our Father . . .

Answer the Call (30107513) © 2011, Tom Kendzia. Published by OCP, 5536 NE Hassalo, Portland, OR 97213. All rights reserved.

Living Faith at Home

"You shall love the Lord, your God, with all your heart, with all your soul, and with all your mind. . . . You shall love your neighbor as yourself."

MATTHEW 22:37, 39

Take a few minutes to reflect on the Scripture art. Ask God to open your eyes and your heart. What feelings are you experiencing? What kinds of expressions do you see on the faces of those listening to Jesus? What do you suppose they are thinking? What else do you notice about the image? Pray a silent prayer of gratitude.

Growing in Faith Together

Help your child to appreciate and treasure the gift of God's love and his law. Look at each faith message below. Together, explore and share the joy of obeying God's commandments. Share from your heart, and listen for the beauty and truth your child holds. Take some quality time together.

The commandments help us to live as children of God, or God's holy people. We follow and obey God's commandments by loving and praising God and by respecting ourselves and others. When we live out Jesus' Great Commandment, we follow and obey all God's commandments.

✝ Invite each family member to choose one of the Ten Commandments on page 91. Then reread together the Great Commandment on page 10. Talk about why following your chosen commandment is also following the Great Commandment.

God allows us to choose to love and honor him and to respect ourselves and others. God also gives us the grace to do what he commands. When we do not do what God commands, he is ready to forgive us if we are sorry.

✝ Hold your child's hands and pray together the Lord's Prayer. At the end of the prayer, encourage your child to forgive, in his or her heart, anyone who needs forgiveness, and do the same yourself. Emphasize the statement "Forgive us our trespasses as we forgive those who trespass against us." Talk about why it is hard to forgive sometimes.

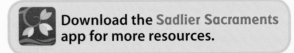

Download the Sadlier Sacraments app for more resources.

CHAPTER 2

Remembering God's Forgiveness

"The LORD is my shepherd."

—Psalm 23:1

Believe

Open Your Heart

Tell about a time when you lost something that was important to you.

How did you feel?

_____

_____

_____

What did you do?

_____

_____

_____

What happened in the end?

_____

_____

_____

God's Love Finds Us

When you choose to do something you know is wrong or hurtful, you lose something very important. You harm your friendship with God and others. It can feel like a piece of your heart is missing. You want back what you have lost.

But God loves us, even when this happens. If we are sorry and ask for forgiveness, God forgives us and puts everything back together again. He can always make our hearts new again.

God makes our hearts new again in the sacraments. The **sacraments** are special signs given to us by Jesus through which we share in God's life and love.

"**I will give them a heart with which to understand that I am the LORD.**"

JEREMIAH 24:7

Complete this sentence: God's love is like . . .

_____

_____

_____

Believe

The Word of the Lord

Jesus told stories to teach people about God's love. He told stories that people could understand so that they could change their ways. One day Jesus told this story.

 Based on LUKE 15:4–6

There was a shepherd who took care of a flock of one hundred sheep. One day one of the sheep wandered away from the flock.

When the shepherd found out the sheep was missing, he left the other ninety-nine sheep. He searched and searched until he found the lost sheep. The shepherd was very happy that he found the lost sheep. He carried it home on his shoulders.

When the shepherd reached home, he called together his friends and neighbors. He said, "Rejoice with me because I have found my lost sheep" (Luke 15:6).

Jesus told this story to help his followers to understand that God loves us and forgives us. He wanted us to know that each one of us is very special to God.

Celebrate

Reconciliation

God loves each of us very much. He wants us to stay as close to him as possible. But this is not always easy to do.

The Scripture story about Adam and Eve teaches us that the first humans did something they knew was wrong. They sinned and lost their share in God's life. And ever since then, all humans are born with **Original Sin**. Because of Adam's Sin, suffering and death came into the world. Also, because of Original Sin, people sometimes find it difficult to do what God wants.

Sometimes we do not show our love for God, others, and ourselves. We hurt others and ourselves. We choose not to follow and obey God's commandments. We sin. **Sin** is any thought, word, or action that we freely choose to do even though we know that it is wrong. Sin is a way of saying "no" to God and God's love.

CATHOLIC IDENTITY
God loved us first.

When we sin, we turn away from God and one another. But Jesus said, "I am the good shepherd" (John 10:14). Jesus, our Good Shepherd, leads us to **reconciliation** with God and others. The word *reconciliation* comes from a word that means "coming back together again." Jesus leads us by showing us ways to come back together again.

Jesus gives us ways to receive God's **forgiveness**. The first way we receive and celebrate God's forgiveness is in the Sacrament of Baptism. Either we are placed in water, or water is poured over us. We become members of the Church and receive a share in God's life. God's life in us is called grace.

In Baptism, Original Sin is taken away. Through the waters of Baptism, we become children of God and members of the Church. The gift of grace that we receive in the sacraments is **sanctifying grace**. Grace is also at work in our daily lives through **actual grace**.

In an emergency, anyone can baptize by pouring water over the head of the one being baptized while saying, "N., I baptize you in the name of the Father, and of the Son, and of the Holy Spirit." The person baptizing must have the intention to baptize as the Church does.

27

Celebrate

Penance and Reconciliation

The new life of grace, received in Baptism, can be weakened or lost by sin. Sins are different from mistakes and accidents. You can make a mistake on a test or bump into a friend by accident. These are *not* sins. But if you cheated on a test or hurt a friend on purpose, that would be different. These actions would be sins, and you would need to seek God's forgiveness for them. We ask for God's forgiveness in Penance and Reconciliation. This sacrament has many names:

- *Sacrament of Penance.* The priest gives us a **penance**, a prayer to say or an action to do that shows sorrow for our sins.

- *sacrament of conversion.* **Conversion** is turning back to God. This is also called *repentance*.

- *sacrament of confession.* **Confession** is the act of telling our sins to the priest in the sacrament.

- *sacrament of forgiveness.* God forgives our sins through the words and actions of the priest. This is called **absolution**.

The word *absolution* comes from a word that means "taking away." When we receive absolution, our sins are taken away. The priest forgives our sins in the name of Jesus Christ.

- *Sacrament of Reconciliation.* We are *reconciled* with God, the Church, and others.

Some sins are more serious than others. These are called **mortal sins**. To commit a mortal sin, a person knows it is very seriously wrong and freely chooses to commit it anyway. Mortal sin breaks our friendship with God and turns us away from him. We no longer share in God's grace.

Venial sin is less serious than mortal sin. Venial sin weakens our friendship with God. But we still share in God's grace.

Any sin that we commit hurts us as well as our friendship with God and others. We should ask for God's forgiveness for all of our sins in the Sacrament of Penance. God shows us his **mercy**, or his love and forgiveness, in the Sacrament of Penance. He calls us back to himself. Children who are baptized as infants must celebrate this sacrament before receiving their First Holy Communion.

A penance is a prayer or an action that shows sorrow for our sins.

Live

Become What You Believe

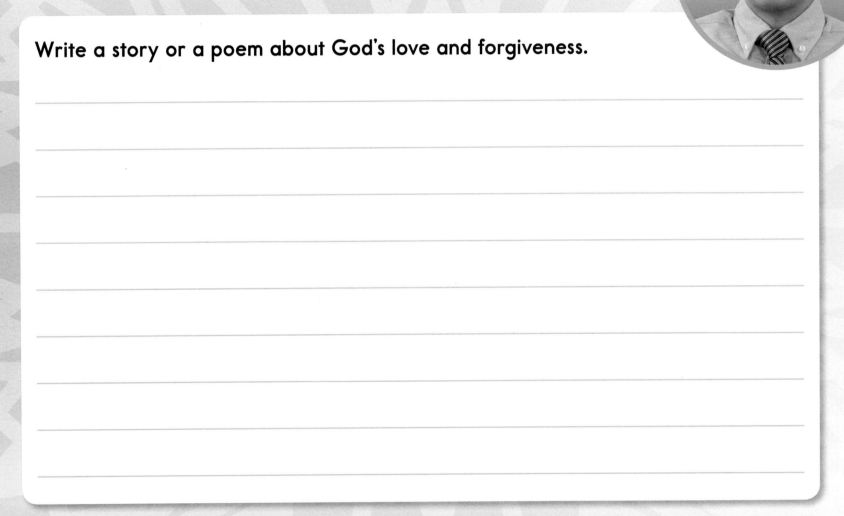

Write a story or a poem about God's love and forgiveness.

I make good choices, and I live in God's love!

Discipleship in Action

Saint Bernadette (1844–1879)

Saint Bernadette Soubirous was born in France to a poor family. She was often sick. The Sisters of Charity taught her in school. When she was fourteen, Bernadette was gathering firewood for her family at a grotto, or cave, outside of Lourdes, France, and she saw the Blessed Mother appear. The Blessed Mother appeared to Bernadette a total of eighteen times. She asked that a church be built. She also spoke to Bernadette about the importance of prayer, conversion, and penance. A spring of water rose up by the grotto, and those who went to it were healed in many ways. Bernadette joined the community of the Sisters of Charity and lived a happy and holy life. Today many people travel to the shrine of Our Lady of Lourdes for healing.

I can show the importance of prayer, conversion, and penance by . . .

Live

Remember Your Love

Leader: Let us begin with the Sign of the Cross and then sing together "Remember Your Love."

All: (*Refrain*) Remember your love and your faithfulness, O Lord. Remember your people, and have mercy on us, Lord.

(*Listen to verses one through three. After each verse, sing the refrain.*)

Leader: O God, help us to remember how much you love us. You sent us your Son, Jesus, who died to forgive our sins, and you sent us your Holy Spirit to help spread your love and forgiveness to everyone in the world.

Filled with God's love, his forgiveness, and his Spirit, let us share a sign of peace.

Let us fold our hands and pray with the words that Jesus taught us.

All: Our Father . . .

Living Faith at ome

"Rejoice with me because I have found my lost sheep."

LUKE 15:6

Take a few minutes to reflect on the Scripture art. Ask God to open your eyes and your heart. What feelings are you experiencing? What do you think the shepherd is feeling or thinking? What else do you notice? Pray a silent prayer of gratitude.

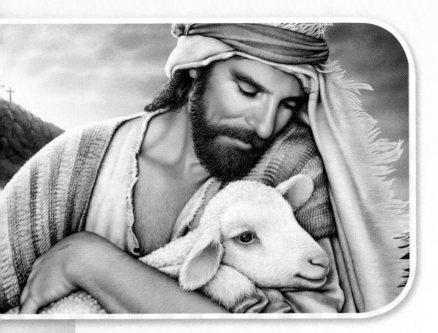

Growing in Faih Together

Help your child to understand the importance of our choices and of seeking God's forgiveness for sins. Look at each faith message below. Then together explore and share the joy of God's love and mercy in your life today. Share from your heart, and listen for the beauty and truth your child holds. Take some quality time together.

When we sin we turn away from God and one another and hurt others and ourselves.

 Think about and name what you can do this week that will build up, not hurt, your friendship with God and others. Do an act of kindness for your child and each person in your family.

God shows his mercy to us in the Sacrament of Penance and Reconciliation. He calls us back to himself.

 Celebrate the Sacrament of Penance and Reconciliation! Receive this sacrament and tell your child why God's mercy is something to be celebrated.

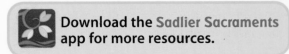

Download the Sadlier Sacraments app for more resources.

Celebrating God's Forgiveness

"May God open your hearts to his law."

—*Rite of Penance*

Believe

Open Your Heart

When I am sorry . . .

I can say:

_____

_____

_____

_____

_____

_____

I can do:

_____

_____

_____

_____

_____

_____

A Closer Look

Have you ever looked through sunglasses, 3D glasses, eyeglasses, or a magnifying glass? How did this change what you saw?

We need to look at the choices we make each day. It is like putting on a pair of glasses to *examine*, or look closely at, what we have thought, said, or done. This will help us to know if we have sinned. When we sin, we can seek God's forgiveness, with sorrow in our hearts.

God will always forgive me when I am really sorry.

Complete this sentence: God's forgiveness is like . . .

Believe

The Word of the Lord

Jesus told this story to help us to understand God's love and forgiveness.

 Based on LUKE 15:11–32

There was a loving father who had two sons. One day the younger son asked for his share of the family's money. The father gave it to him. The son left home. He spent all his money with his friends. When it was gone, he had no place to live and no money to buy clothes or food.

The son thought about his selfish choices. He remembered his father's love. He decided to go home and ask his father for forgiveness. When he was almost home, his father saw him on the road and ran out to welcome him. The young man said, "Father, I have sinned . . . I no longer deserve to be called your son" (Luke 15:21). The father was very happy to see his son. He loved and forgave his son. The father held a feast for his son and said, "We must celebrate and rejoice, because . . . he was lost and has been found" (Luke 15:32).

Examination of Conscience

In Jesus' story about the father and son, the son was not happy or peaceful. After he spent all his money, he thought about the choices he had made. He knew that many of his choices were selfish.

We, too, should think about whether or not our choices show love for God, others, and ourselves. When we do this, we make an **examination of conscience**. As we prepare to celebrate the Sacrament of Penance, we learn how to make an examination of conscience.

When we make an examination of conscience, we do the following:

- We ask the Holy Spirit to help us remember the choices we have made.

- We think about the ways we have or have not followed and obeyed the Ten Commandments.

God loves us as his children and forgives us.

- We ask ourselves if we have hurt others on purpose.

- We ask ourselves if there were times we could have done something good for others but did not.

Here are some questions you can ask when you examine your conscience.

Reverence for God:

- Did I take time to pray?

- Do I go to Mass on Sundays and other Holy Days?

- Did I speak God's name and the names of Jesus, Mary, and all the saints only with honor and praise?

Respect for Myself:

- Did I take care of my body?

- Did I give thanks for my family, friends, and all those who love me?

Respect for Others:

- Did I obey my parents and all those who take care of me?

- Did I hurt other people by what I said or did?

- Did I act with honesty?

- Did I look for ways to help others?

We prepare for the Sacrament of Penance by making an examination of conscience.

CATHOLIC IDENTITY
Grace is the help God gives us.

41

Celebrate

Act of Contrition

In Jesus' story about the father and son, the son felt sorrow for the wrong choices he had made. Another word for sorrow is **contrition**.

We pray a special prayer to tell God that we are sorry for the wrong choices we have made. We call this prayer an **Act of Contrition**. We pray an Act of Contrition during the Sacrament of Penance and Reconciliation.

Before the Sacrament of Penance and Reconciliation, we carefully examine our conscience. We should feel safe to confess all of our sins that we remember. We must always confess mortal sin.

Here is one Act of Contrition that we can pray. You can prepare for the sacrament by learning this prayer.

Act of Contrition

My God,
I am sorry for my sins with
  all my heart.
In choosing to do wrong
and failing to do good,
I have sinned against you
whom I should love above all things.
I firmly intend, with your help,
to do penance,
to sin no more,
and to avoid whatever leads me to sin.
Our Savior Jesus Christ
suffered and died for us.
In his name, my God, have mercy.

We should also confess any venial sins we have remembered.

When we pray these words from the Act of Contrition, this is what we are telling God:
- "firmly intend"—We really mean to do what we promise.
- "do penance"—We will do something to make up for the wrong choices we have made.
- "have mercy"—We ask for God's love and forgiveness.

Live

Become What You Believe

Make your own examination of conscience. Write questions to ask yourself. Then write a prayer to ask God to help you to remember the choices you made, for which you need his mercy.

Questions

_____

_____

_____

_____

_____

Prayer

_____

_____

_____

_____

_____

I trust that God is always with me!

Discipleship in Action

Saint Thomas More (1478–1535)

Sir Thomas More was a very smart and respected lawyer in England in the 1500s. He was also faithful to God's law and the Catholic Church. The King of England chose Thomas to serve on his court. But when the king declared that he himself, not the pope, was the head of the Church in England, Thomas would not support him. Thomas refused to take an oath accepting the king as the leader. Thomas believed it was more important to follow his conscience and do what was right. Thomas was jailed and put on trial for treason. He was found guilty and put to death. Before he died, he said he was the "king's good servant, but God's first."

Following my conscience is important because . . .

Live

Change Our Hearts

Leader: Let us begin with the Sign of the Cross and then sing together "Change Our Hearts."

All: (*Refrain*) Change our hearts this time, your word says it can be. Change our minds this time, your life could make us free. We are the people your call set apart, Lord, this time change our hearts.

Leader: Have I loved God in my mind, in my heart, and in my actions? Have I honored God by participating in the celebration of the Eucharist on Sundays?

All: (*Sing refrain.*)

Leader: Have I been dishonest and not told the truth? Have I been mean to others? Have I hurt my friends?

All: (*Sing refrain.*)

Leader: Let us pray together an Act of Contrition.

All: (*Pray the Act of Contrition on page 43.*)

Leader: Let us offer each other a sign of peace.

Living Faith at ome

"Father, I have sinned."

LUKE 15:21

Take a few minutes to reflect on the Scripture art. Ask God to open your eyes and your heart. What feelings are you experiencing? What does the art tell you about the father and the son? What else do you see? Pray a silent prayer of gratitude.

Growing in Fai✝h Together

Help your child to appreciate and treasure the gift of God's forgiveness. Look at each faith message below. Then, together explore and share the meaning of reconciliation for your family. Share from your heart, and listen for the beauty and truth your child holds. Take some quality time together.

We prepare for the Sacrament of Penance and Reconciliation by making an examination of conscience.

✝ Assist your child in examining his or her choices at the end of each day. As part of bedtime prayers, for example, ask your child to think about his or her words, actions, or thoughts that day; what motivated these; and what he or she feels sorry about and needs God's forgiveness for.

We pray an Act of Contrition during the Sacrament of Penance and Reconciliation. In this prayer we express sorrow for our sins.

✝ Together pray an Act of Contrition (page 43) as part of this bedtime ritual.

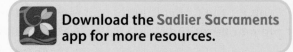
Download the Sadlier Sacraments app for more resources.

Preparing to Celebrate Reconciliation

CHAPTER 4

"May the Lord guide your hearts."

—Rite of Penance

Believe

Open Your Heart

Think of friends, parents, teachers, and others who help and guide you each day. List them below.

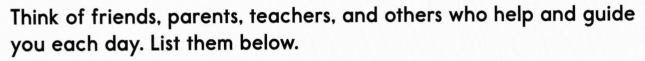

Helping Hands Honor Roll

A Guiding Light

Sometimes we feel afraid or get lost in the dark. We turn on a light or use a flashlight to find our way. In the darkness we feel unsure about what we can't see. We can also experience other kinds of "darkness." For example, we can be unsure about our choices. We can make a wrong choice and not know how to make it right. We can be like lost ships that need a lighthouse to guide our way to shore.

The Holy Spirit always lights our way. Scripture says:

"The LORD is my light and my salvation;
   whom do I fear?" (Psalm 27:1)

The Holy Spirit guides us, helping us to make the right choices. God shines his light of forgiveness on us when we are truly sorry for our sins or the wrong choices we have made.

How do you show forgiveness to others?

With the guidance of the Holy Spirit, Christ entrusted to his Apostles the ministry of reconciliation.

—Based on *Catechism of the Catholic Church*, 1461

Believe

The Word of the Lord

Large crowds often gathered to see Jesus and listen to his teachings. Jesus welcomed everyone to hear the Good News about his Father.

 Based on LUKE 19:1–10

One day a crowd gathered to see Jesus. Zacchaeus, a dishonest tax collector, was in the crowd. He wanted to see Jesus but was too short to see over the crowd. So, he climbed a sycamore tree and waited. As Jesus walked by the tree, he looked up. He said, "Zacchaeus, come down quickly, for today I must stay at your house" (Luke 19:5).

Zacchaeus climbed down. He welcomed Jesus to his home. This angered some people. They thought Zacchaeus had cheated them. They did not know why Jesus would visit him.

Zacchaeus told Jesus that he would pay back four times the amount of money he owed to people. He would give half of what he owned to the poor. By his words and actions he showed that he was really sorry. Jesus told him he was saved.

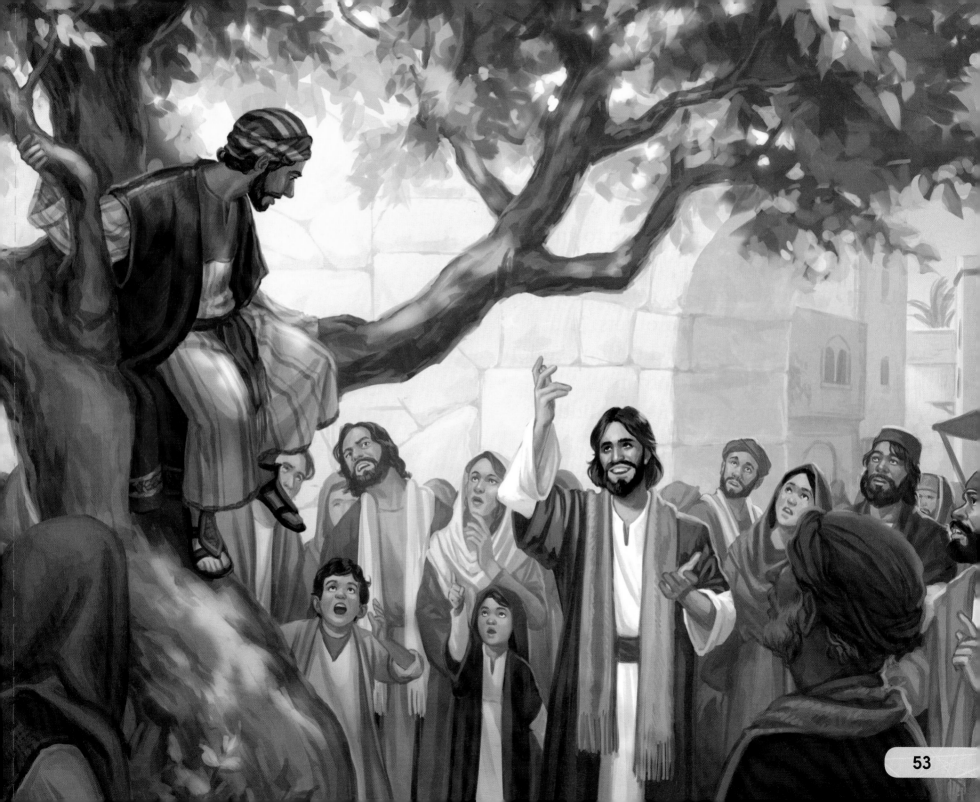

Celebrate

The Sacrament of Forgiveness

When Jesus traveled from town to town, he shared God's love with people. He forgave their sins in God's name. He celebrated their reconciliation with God and others. Jesus gave us a way to celebrate our reconciliation with God, the Church, and others: the Sacrament of Penance and Reconciliation.

When we celebrate this sacrament, we meet with a priest. We may sit and face the priest or kneel behind a screen. The priest may read Scripture with us. He talks to us about what we can do to make right choices and live the way Jesus taught us. We tell God we are sorry for our sins and promise not to sin again. This is how we express contrition. Perfect contrition is being sorry for our sins because we believe in God and love him.

The Sacrament of Penance reconciles us with God and the Church.

When we tell our sins to the priest, we are confessing our sins to God. This is called *confession*. The priest is never allowed to tell anyone the sins that we confess. This is the *seal of confession*.

The priest tells us ways we can show God we are sorry. The priest tells us to pray certain prayers. He may also tell us to do a kind act for others. The prayers or kind act are called an *act of penance*. Through our act of penance, we show God we are sorry, repair the harm caused by our sins, and express how we will try our best to make better choices as disciples of Jesus. Acts of penance are also called acts of satisfaction.

Zacchaeus promised Jesus that he would show God he was sorry for his sins. We, too, show God that we are sorry for our sins by doing the penance that the priest gives us. We do our penance right after the celebration of the sacrament.

The Sacrament of Penance and Reconciliation has four parts: contrition, confession, an act of penance, and absolution.

We are reconciled with God and the Church by confessing our sins to the priest and receiving forgiveness within the Sacrament of Penance.

Celebrate

Receiving Absolution

After Jesus rose from the dead, he returned to his Apostles and gave them the power to forgive sin in his name. And today, in the Sacrament of Penance and Reconciliation, bishops and priests forgive our sins in Jesus' name. They received this power in the Sacrament of Holy Orders.

God forgives our sins through the words and actions of the priest in the Sacrament of Penance. The words of absolution that the priest prays promise us that God forgives our sins. To receive absolution is to be freed from our sins. The priest forgives our sins in Jesus' name.

Only bishops and priests, who receive the power to forgive sins in Jesus' name in Holy Orders, can absolve us of our sins.

After we say an Act of Contrition, the priest says the words of absolution. He stretches his right hand over our head and prays:

"God, the Father of mercies,
through the death and resurrection
  of his Son
has reconciled the world to himself
and sent the Holy Spirit among us
for the forgiveness of sins;
through the ministry of the Church
may God give you pardon and peace,
and I absolve you from your sins
in the name of the Father,
  and of the Son, †
and of the Holy Spirit."

We respond, "Amen."

Live

Become What You Believe

In the Sacrament of Penance and Reconciliation the priest may tell us to do a kind act for our penance. What is one kind act you can do for each of the people below?

Friend:

_____

_____

_____

_____

_____

Family Member:

_____

_____

_____

_____

_____

Teacher:

_____

_____

_____

_____

_____

God will always forgive me when I am sorry!

Discipleship in Action

Saint Theodora (1798–1856)

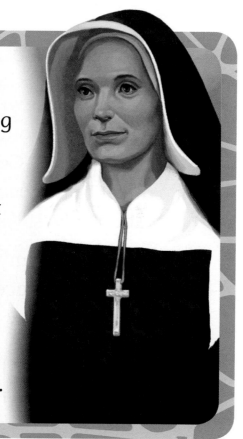

Theodora was born in France and named Anne-Thérèse. Growing up, she had a strong faith in God. On the day of her First Holy Communion she told the priest she wanted to be a nun. At age twenty-four, she joined the Sisters of Providence. The bishop sent her and five other sisters to Saint Mary-of-the-Woods, Indiana, as missionaries. The sisters began a new community under her leadership. They had many hard times. But Mother Theodora, as she was known, told them to trust in God's care and protection. Her religious community helped the sick, poor, and orphans of the community. Today they serve in many other places in the world.

I can trust in God's care and protection in my life when . . .

Live

Open My Eyes

Leader: Let us begin with the Sign of the Cross. Bless our eyes. Help us to see your face, O God, in everyone we meet and especially when we look at ourselves.

All: (*Sing*) Open my eyes, Lord. Help me to see your face.

Open my eyes, Lord. Help me to see.

Leader: Bless our ears. Help us to hear your voice, O God, in the words of our parents and friends when they help us and show us how to live.

All: (*Sing*) Open my ears, Lord. Help me to hear your voice.

Open my ears, Lord. Help me to hear.

Leader: Bless our hearts. Help us to seek your forgiveness, O God, as we prepare our hearts to be filled with your love and kindness. Only when we are one with you in forgiveness and love can we share the love of Jesus, your Son.

All: (*Sing*) Open my heart, Lord. Help me to love like you.
Open my heart, Lord. Help me to love.
I live within you, deep in your heart, O Love.
I live within you. Rest now in me.

Leader: Our Father . . .

Living Faith at 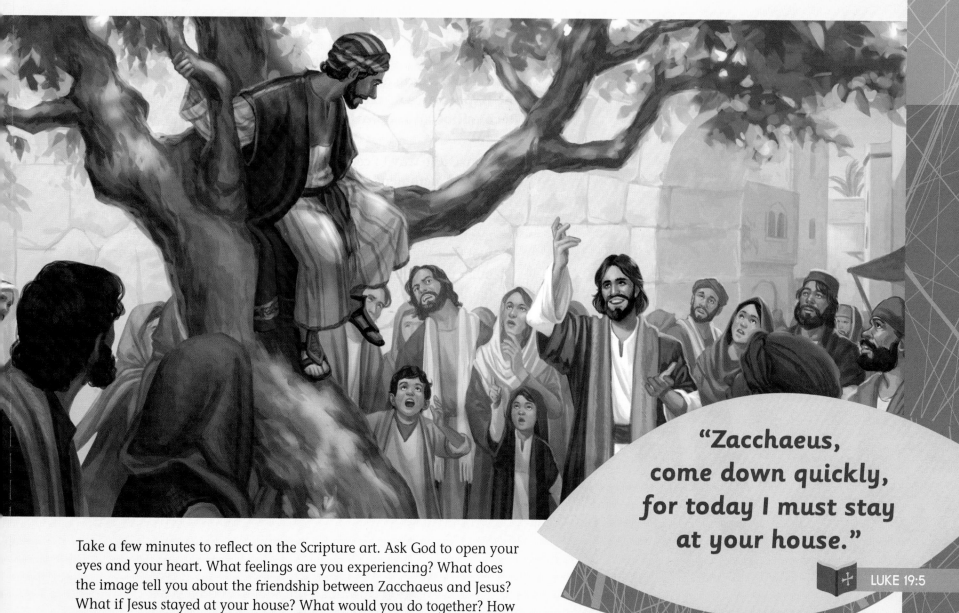Home

"Zacchaeus, come down quickly, for today I must stay at your house."

LUKE 19:5

Take a few minutes to reflect on the Scripture art. Ask God to open your eyes and your heart. What feelings are you experiencing? What does the image tell you about the friendship between Zacchaeus and Jesus? What if Jesus stayed at your house? What would you do together? How would you make him feel at home? Pray a silent prayer of gratitude.

Growing in Fai✝h Together

Help your child to appreciate and treasure the blessings of the Catholic faith. Look at each faith message below. Share from your heart, and listen for the beauty and truth your child holds. Take some quality time together. Explore and share the importance of receiving the Sacrament of Penance and Reconciliation regularly.

Jesus gave us a way to celebrate our reconciliation with God and others: the Sacrament of Penance and Reconciliation.

✝ With your child suggest words to describe the feeling of being reconciled with another person, such as *peace* and *friendship*. Pray that God will always help and guide your family so that peace and other positive experiences fill your family life. Discuss how your family can become better at forgiving one another.

The Sacrament of Penance and Reconciliation has four parts: contrition, confession, an act of penance, and absolution.

✝ Review with your child what happens in each part of the Sacrament of Penance and Reconciliation, using this chapter as a reference. Encourage your child to be joyful and thankful about the gift of God's forgiveness that we celebrate in this sacrament.

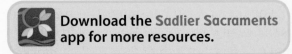

Download the Sadlier Sacraments app for more resources.

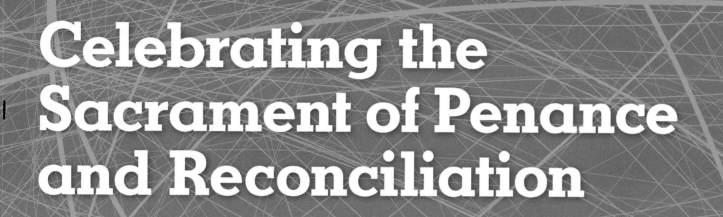

Celebrating the Sacrament of Penance and Reconciliation

CHAPTER 5

"Hear us, Lord, for you are merciful and kind."

—Rite of Penance

Believe

Open Your Heart

Remember a time when you had a change of heart. For example, after thinking or acting one way toward someone or something, you realized you were wrong. Tell your story below in three parts. Draw a picture for each part.

1. What I Thought or Did at First

_____

_____

2. What Made Me Have a Change of Heart

_____

_____

3. What I Did to Show My Change of Heart

_____

_____

God's Love Is Always Shining

The world around us is always changing. Some changes are small and hard to see. Others are big and amazing, like the rising and setting of the sun. When the sun sets, the earth is really turning away from the sun. The sun's light has to travel farther. The sun's color changes, first to orange, then to red. These are just the rays of light that can travel the farthest. The next day, the earth turns back toward the sun. The full light of the sun shines on us again. It is a new day.

People can also change. People might turn away from God's love, but every day is a new day with God! When we come back to God, and are truly sorry and want to do better, he forgives us. He always gives us another chance.

What is it like when someone gives you another chance?

We all need God's love and forgiveness.

Believe

The Word of the Lord

In Jesus' time, when people had guests come to their homes, they would ask the servants to wash their guests' feet because they were dirty from walking on dirt roads.

 Based on LUKE 7:36–50

One day a man named Simon invited Jesus to dinner. But when Jesus entered the house, no one offered to wash his feet.

During dinner a woman from the town came in and knelt by Jesus at the table. The woman cried so hard that her tears washed the dirt from Jesus' feet. Simon thought she was a sinner. He asked Jesus why he had let a sinner wash his feet.

Jesus answered, "When I entered your house, you did not give me water for my feet, but she has bathed them with her tears. . . . So I tell you, her many sins have been forgiven" (Luke 7:44, 47).

Then Jesus said to the woman, "Your sins are forgiven. . . . Your faith has saved you; go in peace" (Luke 7:48, 50).

Celebrate

Communal Celebration

At special times of the year our parish community gathers to celebrate the Sacrament of Penance together. We celebrate the sacrament in a **communal celebration with individual confession**. This is what we do:

We gather and sing a hymn together. Then the priest welcomes us.

- We listen to readings from Scripture about God's love and forgiveness.

- The priest talks to us about the readings.

- We listen to questions that are part of an examination of conscience. We think about our sins and the choices we have made.

In the communal celebration of the Sacrament of Penance, we pray an Act of Contrition together. We individually confess our sins, accept a penance, and receive absolution.

- We pray an Act of Contrition together. We tell God we are sorry for our sins and that we will try not to sin again. We pray the Lord's Prayer. Each penitent privately tells his or her sins to the priest.

- The priest tells each penitent to do an act of penance.

- The priest prays the words of absolution by stretching his right hand over each penitent's head and saying the words of absolution. The priest forgives each penitent's sins in the name of the Father, the Son, and the Holy Spirit.

- Together we all praise and thank God for his mercy.

- The priest blesses the parish community. He tells all of us, "The Lord has freed you from your sins. Go in peace."

During the Sacrament of Penance, we will see the priest wearing a purple **stole**. The stole is the sign of priestly office. It is worn during all sacramental celebrations. Since purple is a sign of penance, it helps us to remember to show our sorrow for sins by doing the penance the priest gives us.

Celebrate

Individual Celebration

Here is what happens when you celebrate the Sacrament of Penance in **individual confession** alone, without a communal celebration:

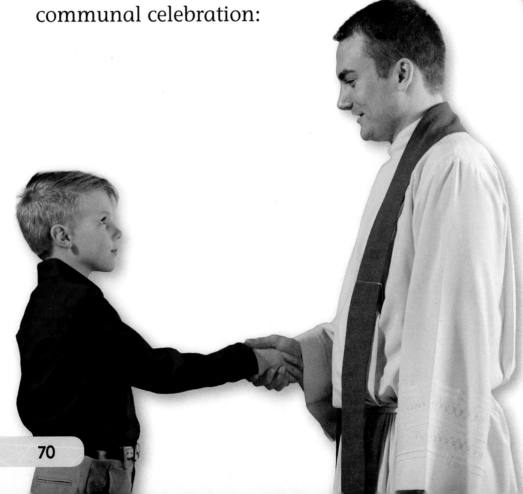

- The priest welcomes you, and you both make the Sign of the Cross.

- You listen as the priest reads a Scripture story about God's forgiveness.

- You confess your sins to the priest.

- You and the priest talk about making right choices.

- The priest gives you an act of penance. You will do your penance after the celebration of the sacrament.

- You pray an Act of Contrition. You tell God you are sorry for your sins and that you will try not to sin again.

- The priest prays the words of absolution, stretching his right hand over your head. In the name of the Father, the Son, and the Holy Spirit your sins are forgiven by the priest.

- You and the priest praise and thank God for his love and forgiveness.

- The priest tells you, "The Lord has freed you from your sins. Go in peace."

In individual confession, we confess our sins to the priest, accept a penance from the priest, pray an Act of Contrition, and receive absolution.

Through the Sacrament of Holy Orders, a man becomes a priest. Many priests serve in local parishes. Priests spend their lives sharing God's love with people. They act in the person of Christ in celebrating Mass and other sacraments.

Live

Become What You Believe

How do I give other people another chance?

To show others I have forgiven them, I have . . .

_____

_____

_____

To be more forgiving this week, I will . . .

_____

_____

_____

God forgives my sins through the Church in the Sacrament of Penance and Reconciliation!

Discipleship in Action

Saint Cyprian (A.D. 200–258)

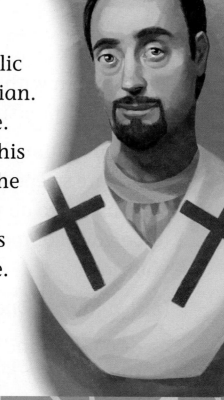

Saint Cyprian was born during the early centuries of the Catholic Church in North Africa. His family was wealthy and not Christian. As an adult Cyprian became a Christian and changed his life. He gave money to the poor and promised to live a holy life. This great change of heart amazed his community. Two years later he was ordained a priest and, soon after, a bishop. As a bishop Saint Cyprian called people to turn away from their sinful ways and come back to the Church after a period of public penance. His practices helped to shape the way the Church celebrates the Sacrament of Penance and Reconciliation. Saint Cyprian died as a martyr for his faith.

I can lead others to have a change of heart and turn back to God by . . .

Live

Healing Balm

Leader: Let us begin with the Sign of the Cross and then sing together.

All: (*Refrain*) Healing balm we shall be, for we are steeped in your mercy. Send us out to do your will, O God: to be your compassion and your love.

(*Listen to verse one.*)

Gentle God, kind and true,
You are the source of all that is good . . .

(*Sing refrain.*)

(*Listen to verse two.*)

Gracious God, we blossom anew, fed by the rain of your endless love . . .

(*Sing refrain.*)

(*Listen to verse three.*)

Healing God, give us strength to be fountains of justice . . .

(*Sing refrain.*)

Leader: Let us offer one another a sign of peace and pray as Jesus taught us.

All: Our Father . . .

Living Faith at ome

"Your sins are forgiven. . . . Your faith has saved you; go in peace."

LUKE 7:48, 50

Take a few minutes to reflect on the Scripture art. Ask God to open your eyes and your heart. What feelings are you experiencing? What does this image tell you about Jesus? What else do you see? Pray a silent prayer of gratitude.

Growing in Fai✝h Together

Help your child to appreciate and treasure the blessings of the Catholic faith. Look at each faith message below. Share from your heart, and listen for the beauty and truth your child holds. Take some quality time together.

God's love is always active and present in our lives. God always gives us a chance to turn away from sin. Through the Church we experience forgiveness for our sins in the Sacrament of Penance and Reconciliation.

 Share some examples of times each of you has been forgiving. Share examples of times each of you has experienced forgiveness. What allowed forgiveness in each of these situations?

Through the power of the Holy Spirit and the ministry of the priest, our sins are forgiven in the Sacrament of Penance and Reconciliation. Priests act in the person of Christ in celebrating the sacraments.

 Show appreciation for your parish priest. Send him a thoughtful note or message thanking him for his ministry.

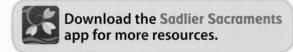
Download the Sadlier Sacraments app for more resources.

Living God's Peace

CHAPTER 6

"Make us living signs of your love for the whole world to see."

—*Rite of Penance*

Believe

Open Your Heart

Think of ways people live and work together in peace. Draw a picture that shows an example of when you felt peaceful.

Spreading God's Peace

Think about what happens when you drop a stone into the water: ripples of water form near the center and then spread out. Spreading the peace of Christ is like that. The peace you receive from Jesus Christ begins in your heart. And you can share his peace with others.

> **"Lord, make me an instrument of your peace."**
> —*Prayer of Saint Francis*

When you show understanding or care to a family member, you can help your whole family feel more peaceful. When you forgive a friend, you can help build more peaceful relationships among all your friends. All your caring actions have effects. They show that you have respect for others. Each time you show love and respect for others, you share God's peace and help others know God is with them.

How do you bring peace and joy to your family and friends?

Believe

The Word of the Lord

One day a very large crowd of people gathered to see Jesus. Jesus went up to the top of a mountain to teach. He knew that doing this would help everyone in the crowd to see and hear him.

 Based on MATTHEW 5:1–2, 9

Jesus said that day,
"Blessed are the peacemakers,
for they will be called children of God"

(Matthew 5:9).

Jesus told us that he wants us to be peacemakers, too. We are peacemakers when we ask others to forgive us. We are also peacemakers when we show forgiveness, patience, kindness, and honesty toward others.

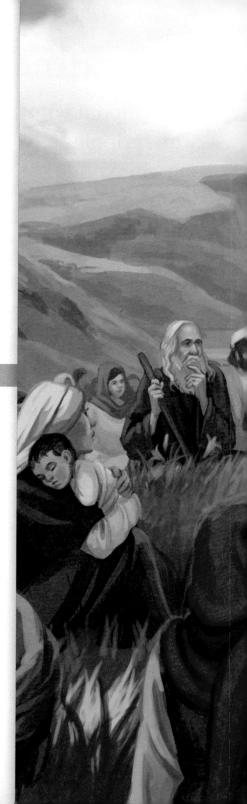

Celebrate

Forgiveness and Peace

At the end of the celebration of the Sacrament of Penance and Reconciliation, the priest tells us, "Go in peace." We go in peace because our sins are forgiven. Then, as soon as we can, we do the act of penance the priest has given us. Remember, the penance may be to say a prayer or prayers. The penance may also be to do an act of kindness. When we do our penance, we show that we are sorry for our sins and want to do better.

Through the Sacrament of Penance:

- our sins are forgiven
- we are reconciled to God and to the Church
- we experience peace and comfort
- the gift of God's grace is strengthened in us.

CATHOLIC IDENTITY
Joy is a gift from the Holy Spirit and a sign that God is with us.

Doing a kind act as a penance shows that we are sorry for our sins.

On the night before he died, Jesus said, "Peace I leave with you; my peace I give to you" (John 14:27).

On that same night, Jesus also promised his disciples that the Holy Spirit would come to be their helper. The Holy Spirit came to the Church on Pentecost. God the Holy Spirit is with the Church to guide us.

The Holy Spirit helps us to spread love and peace to others, as Jesus did. **Catholic social teaching** is the teaching of the Church that calls all members to work for justice and peace as Jesus did. This Church teaching reminds us that we are all God's children. It teaches us ways to love and respect all people. As disciples of Jesus, we try to build a world of peace and justice.

We are all
God's children.

Celebrate

Showing Love and Respect

Jesus taught us that each person is a gift from God. We are to help people who are in need. **Works of Mercy** are things we can do to help care for the needs of others. There are Corporal Works of Mercy and Spiritual Works of Mercy. The Works of Mercy are meant to help people receive the things they need. For example, we all need food, water, and clothing. We also need a place to live. And when we are sick, we need caring people to help us feel better.

There are Works of Mercy that help people in other ways. We share God's peace when we are patient and forgiving. And with a smile or a kind word, we can comfort someone who is sad or lonely. Jesus also taught us to pray for the needs of others.

By doing Works of Mercy, we share with others the love and peace of Jesus Christ. When we share Christ's peace and love, we help to make the world a happy and peaceful place.

Works of Mercy

Corporal

Feed the hungry.
Give drink to the thirsty.
Clothe the naked.
Visit the imprisoned.
Shelter the homeless.
Visit the sick.
Bury the dead.

Spiritual

Admonish the sinner.
Instruct the ignorant.
Counsel the doubtful.
Comfort the sorrowful.
Bear wrongs patiently.
Forgive all injuries.
Pray for the living and the dead.

Live

Become What You Believe

You are an instrument of God's peace. Write one way you share peace on each sign.

PEACE
this Way →

I can bring God's love and peace to others!

Discipleship in Action

Saint Elizabeth of Portugal (1271–1336)

Saint Elizabeth was the queen of Portugal. She spent most of her time making life better for the people in her kingdom. People who were sick came to her. Elizabeth served them meals and cared for them herself. She gave her money to hospitals and other good causes. Men, women, and children trusted Elizabeth and were thankful for her help. The people saw that their queen was a great peacemaker. She brought peace to her own family. She was able to settle disagreements between kingdoms. Saint Elizabeth said, "God made me queen so that I may serve others."

Draw a picture of yourself being a peacemaker.

Live

I Send You Out

Leader: Let us begin with the Sign of the Cross and then sing together.

All: (*Refrain*) I send you out on a mission of love. (*three times*)
And know that I am with you always until the end of the world.

(*Listen to verse one.*)

I baptize you . . .

(*Sing refrain.*)

(*Listen to verse two.*)

Well, it's time for us . . .

(*Sing refrain.*)

Leader: O God, we pray that you may help us to bring the peace of your forgiveness to our families and friends. You want us to share your love and joy with everyone.
We want to be the light of Christ in the world. Let us go out on a mission of love, to spread the good news that Jesus is life!

All: (*Sing refrain. Repeat.*)

Living Faith at ome

"Blessed are the peacemakers, for they will be called children of God."

MATTHEW 5:9

Take a few minutes to reflect on the Scripture art. Ask God to open your eyes and your heart. What feelings are you experiencing? What in the scene helps you to feel at peace? How are the people responding to Jesus' message about peace? Pray a silent prayer of gratitude.

Growing in Fai✝h Together

Help your child to understand that after we celebrate God's forgiveness, we are freed from our sins. Help your child to appreciate and treasure this and the other blessings of the Catholic faith. Look at each faith message below. Share from your heart, and listen for the beauty and truth your child holds. Take some quality time together.

In the Sacrament of Penance and Reconciliation we encounter the love and mercy of Jesus Christ. God forgives our sins and takes away the punishment for our sins. Experiencing God's mercy and love brings us peace and comfort. God asks us to share his peace and love with others and to try not to sin again.

 Share with each other ways to spread God's peace within your family. Then pray together the prayer of Saint Francis: "Lord, make me an instrument of your peace."

Works of Mercy are kind and caring acts of love. When we practice the Corporal and Spiritual Works of Mercy, we bring God's peace, justice, and love to ourselves and to others.

 With your child, read the Works of Mercy on page 85. Share ways your parish family helps others, such as collecting clothes for families or providing meals for elderly people. Imagine other ways that your family can show God's love to others through caring actions. How can your family connect with a parish ministry to show your love and care for others?

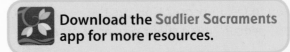
Download the Sadlier Sacraments app for more resources.

The Ten Commandments

	Ways to Follow the Commandments
1. I am the LORD your God: you shall not have strange gods before me.	We believe that there is only one God.
2. You shall not take the name of the LORD your God in vain.	We speak God's name only with love and respect. We honor and respect the names of Jesus, Mary, and all the saints.
3. Remember to keep holy the LORD's Day.	We join our parish each week for Mass on Sunday or Saturday evening and on Holy Days of Obligation.
4. Honor your father and your mother.	We obey our parents and all who care for us.
5. You shall not kill.	We respect all human life.
6. You shall not commit adultery.	We respect our bodies and the bodies of others.
7. You shall not steal.	We take care of what we own and share with those in need.
8. You shall not bear false witness against your neighbor.	We tell the truth.
9. You shall not covet your neighbor's wife.	We show that we are happy and thankful for our family and friends. We are pure of heart and show love in an honest and faithful way.
10. You shall not covet your neighbor's goods.	We show that we are happy and thankful for what we own.

Celebrating the Sacrament of Penance and Reconciliation

Individual Confession

First I examine my conscience.
The priest greets me.
We both make the Sign of the Cross.

The priest asks me to trust in God's mercy.
The priest or I may read from Scripture.

I talk with the priest and I confess my sins.
The priest talks to me about loving God and others.
He gives me an act of penance.
I pray an Act of Contrition.

In the name of God and the Church, the priest grants me absolution:
The priest extends his hand over my head.
Through the words and actions of the priest, I receive God's forgiveness of my sins.

Together the priest and I give thanks for God's forgiveness.

I am sent to go in peace and to do the penance the priest gave me.

Communal Celebration with Individual Confession

We sing an opening hymn.
The priest greets us.
The priest prays an opening prayer.
We listen to a reading from Scripture and a homily.

We listen to questions that help us to examine our conscience.
Together we pray an Act of Contrition.
We may say a prayer or sing a song.
Then we pray the Lord's Prayer.

I meet individually with a priest to confess my sins.
The priest gives me an act of penance.
The priest grants me absolution.

After everyone has met individually with a priest, we thank God together for loving and forgiving us.
The priest says a concluding prayer to thank God.
The priest blesses us.
We are sent to go in peace and do the penance the priest gave to each of us.

Sign of the Cross

In the name of the Father,
and of the Son,
and of the Holy Spirit.
Amen.

Lord's Prayer

Our Father, who art in heaven,
hallowed be thy name;
thy kingdom come;
thy will be done on earth
   as it is in heaven.
Give us this day our daily bread;
and forgive us our trespasses
as we forgive those
   who trespass against us;
and lead us not into temptation,
but deliver us from evil.
Amen.

Glory Be to the Father

Glory be to the Father
and to the Son
and to the Holy Spirit,
as it was in the beginning,
is now, and ever shall be
world without end.
Amen.

Hail Mary

Hail Mary, full of grace,
the Lord is with you!
Blessed are you among women,
and blessed is the fruit
   of your womb, Jesus.
Holy Mary, Mother of God,
pray for us sinners,
now and at the hour of our death.
Amen.

Act of Contrition

My God,
I am sorry for my sins with
  all my heart.
In choosing to do wrong
and failing to do good,
I have sinned against you
whom I should love above all things.
I firmly intend, with your help,
to do penance,
to sin no more,
and to avoid whatever leads me to sin.
Our Savior Jesus Christ
suffered and died for us.
In his name, my God, have mercy.

Prayer for Peace

Lord, make me an instrument of your peace:
where there is hatred, let me sow love;
where there is injury, pardon;
where there is doubt, faith;
where there is despair, hope;
where there is darkness, light;
where there is sadness, joy.

O divine Master, grant that I may not so
  much seek
to be consoled as to console,
to be understood as to understand,
to be loved as to love.
For it is in giving that we receive,
it is in pardoning that we are pardoned,
it is in dying that we are born to eternal life.
Amen.

Saint Francis of Assisi

absolution (page 28) God's forgiveness of sins through the words and actions of the priest in the Sacrament of Penance and Reconciliation

Act of Contrition (page 42) a prayer to tell God that we are sorry for the wrong choices we have made and to promise to try not to sin again

actual grace (page 27) grace at work in our daily lives, helping us to do good

Catholic social teaching (page 83) the teaching of the Church that calls all members to work for justice and peace as Jesus did

communal celebration with individual confession (page 68) the Sacrament of Penance and Reconciliation as celebrated by the parish community gathered together

confession (page 28) the act of telling our sins to the priest in the Sacrament of Penance and Reconciliation

conscience (page 15) God's gift that helps us to know what is right and what is wrong, what to do and what not to do

contrition (page 42) sorrow for sin

conversion (page 28) turning back to God

examination of conscience (page 40) thinking about whether or not our choices show love for God, others, and ourselves

forgiveness (page 27) mercy and pardoning of sin

free will (page 14) God's gift that allows us to make our own choices

grace (page 15) the gift of God's life in us

Great Commandment (page 13) Jesus' teaching about loving God, others, and ourselves

individual confession (page 70) the Sacrament of Penance and Reconciliation as celebrated by an individual with the priest

mercy (page 29) love and forgiveness

moral choice (page 15) a choice between right and wrong, between obeying one of the commandments and not obeying it

mortal sins (page 29) very serious sins that break a person's friendship with God, or turning away from God

Original Sin (page 26) the state of sin and the loss of our share in God's life that we inherit from the sin of Adam and Eve

penance (page 28) a prayer to say or an action to do that shows sorrow for our sins

reconciliation (page 27) the restoring of our friendship and peace with God and others

sacraments (page 23) special signs given to us by Jesus through which we share in God's life and love

sanctifying grace (page 27) the gift of grace that we receive in the sacraments through the power of the Holy Spirit

sin (page 26) any thought, word, or action that we freely choose to do even though we know that it is wrong

stole (page 69) a special garment that the priest wears around the back of his neck, with two ends hanging parallel in front, during all sacramental celebrations, as a sign of his priestly office

Ten Commandments (page 12) Laws given to us by God

venial sin (page 29) less serious sin that weakens a person's friendship with God

Works of Mercy (page 84) things we can do to help care for the needs of others